# EXUDE
# SELF-CONFIDENCE
# IN THE WORKPLACE

A Practical Guide and Workbook

# EXUDE SELF-CONFIDENCE IN THE WORKPLACE

A Practical Guide and Workbook

Alejandro Perez

Published in 2022 by Tamarind Hill Press

Copyright © Alejandro Perez 2022

Alejandro Perez asserts his right to be identified as the author of this work in accordance with the Copyright, Design and Patents Act of 1988.

All rights reserved. No part of this publication may be reproduced, stored in a retrievable system, or transmitted in any form or by any means, electronic, mechanical photocopying, recording or otherwise, without the permission of the author and copyright owner.

ISBN:

**978-1-915161-91-8**

Tamarind Hill Press Limited

Copies are available at special rates for bulk orders. Contact us on email at info@tamarindhillpress.co.uk or by phone on +44 7982 90 90 37 for more information.

**TAMARiND HiLL**
**.PRESS**

# Acknowledgements

This book is dedicated to my younger-self: I want to thank him for enduring when we didn't have the skills to do and be our absolute best. Thank you for sticking with me through it all and for being willing to learn what was necessary to become better. Our future is brighter and life is so much better than it was two years ago. We have been through some tough times, but doing this work was necessary and now so much has improved.

My thanks go to my partner, Angelique. I am grateful that I learned the skills needed so that I was confident in myself to finally ask you out. Thanks for being by my side. It has been an amazing year and I look forward to spending the rest of my life with you.

To Kemone and the THP team, thank you so much for accepting this book for publication. You have all been great to work with. I could not have done this without all your efforts. Thank you.

Stacey, thank you for being a leader and friend. Your leadership techniques make it easy to grow at work. I appreciate your continuous feedback and your method of delivery. I am sure everyone in the department would agree that they can be their best because you allow them to.

I couldn't have achieved anything I have without the love and support of my family. Thank you all for nurturing my talents and natural way of being. I am grateful that you all allowed me to come out of my shell in my own time. For all that you have invested in me, especially my dear mother, thank you. I am blessed to have all of you in my life and on this journey.

To my colleagues, lecturers, trainers, friends—all current and past—who have helped me in one way or another, thank you.

# Table of Contents

ACKNOWLEDGEMENTS .................................................................. V

INTRODUCTION ............................................................................ 7

   WHAT EXACTLY IS SELF-CONFIDENCE, AND HOW CAN YOU CULTIVATE IT? .... 10
      *Factors for Lack of Self-confidence* ...................................................... 11
         EXERCISE 1 ........................................................................ 13

   **STRATEGIES TO REVAMP YOUR SELF-CONFIDENCE** ............................. 22
      KEEP YOUR ATTENTION ON YOURSELF. ............................................................ 22
      MAKE THE MOST OF YOUR ASSETS BY RECOGNIZING AND USING THEM. ................... 22
      RECOGNIZE AND ADDRESS YOUR AREAS OF WEAKNESS. ....................................... 23
      HAVE FAITH IN YOUR OWN ABILITIES. ............................................................. 23
      KEEP A CLOSE EYE ON YOUR ACCOMPLISHMENTS ............................................... 23
      KEEP A DIGITAL "KUDOS FILE" OF YOUR ACCOMPLISHMENTS. ............................... 23
      CONFIDENCE MIGHT BE SHAKY AT TIMES, SO BE AWARE OF THIS ........................... 24
      SEEK OUT THE SUPPORT OF OTHERS. ............................................................. 24
      GET FEEDBACK .......................................................................................... 25
      ATTEMPT NEW THINGS. .............................................................................. 25
      YOU SHOULD CULTIVATE AN OPTIMISTIC OUTLOOK. .......................................... 26
      EXERCISE 2 .............................................................................................. 27

**SELF-CONFIDENCE IN THE WORKPLACE: A FEW REAL-WORLD EXAMPLES** ........... 44

**HOW TO BECOME MORE SELF-CONFIDENT AT WORK** ....................... 45
      KEEP AN OPEN MIND AND BE WILLING TO GIVE NEW IDEAS A GO. ........................ 45
      PARTICIPATE FULLY IN THE PROCESS OF EVALUATING YOUR OWN PERFORMANCE. ....... 46
      GIVE YOURSELF SOME BREATHING ROOM BEFORE TAKING ON NEW ENDEAVOURS. .... 46
      DO NOT BE ASHAMED OF YOUR INDIVIDUALITY. ............................................... 46
      MAINTAINING A SENSE OF PERSPECTIVE IS KEY TO ACHIEVING YOUR OBJECTIVES. ...... 46
      ANALYSE THE LANGUAGE YOU USE TO COMMUNICATE TO YOURSELF. ..................... 47
      MAKE FRIENDS WITH YOUR CO-WORKERS. ...................................................... 47
      QUIET YOUR INNER CRITIC. ......................................................................... 47
      TAKE CARE OF YOUR PHYSICAL AND MENTAL HEALTH. ....................................... 47
      DEFINE CONFIDENCE IN TERMS OF WHAT EXACTLY IT MEANS TO YOU. ................... 48
      EXERCISE 3 .............................................................................................. 49

   CONCLUSION ........................................................................... 60

   NOTES ...................................................................................... 62

# Introduction

You are not alone if you have ever felt a lack of self-confidence in your professional life. This is something that many experience at one point or another, no matter how quickly it passes or how long it lasts. For me, I often experienced a lack of self-confidence when it came to preparing reports and presentations for my superiors. I mean, it is expected that they know more than I do and they have the power to fire me if I do not meet their expectations. Added to that, I am an introvert. For someone like me, standing in front of anyone and speaking, all eyes on me, is just not something that I like. As a result, I often found myself hyperventilating before doing a presentation and it is the time when I feel the least confident in my profession. You have probably been there too. However, when I lost my job at the start of the Covid-19 pandemic, I lost all the confidence I had as it relates to my career, not just when it comes to report writing or making verbal presentations.

I had left my role as an accountant almost a year earlier to join this new company as their senior accountant. The pay was better and it was the next step in my career. When I took the job, it was the best decision at the time and, in all honesty, everything was going well, until it wasn't. Working in this new company, I had pretty much found my tribe. I was working in a team with people who understood and appreciated my strengths as much as they accepted my weaknesses.

I am savage when it comes to accounting. I know all there is to know—I am always learning and improving both my knowledge and skills—and I am quick and accurate when I need to be. My memory is like no other. The CEO can be anywhere in the world and ring me while I am asleep to get some form of figures they need and I will have it on hand to give. I love my career and it shows in my work.

The pandemic hit our company hard and this meant that they needed to get rid of people. Unfortunately for me, I was one of three people in this position at the company and the newest, so it was only natural that I would be the first for them to get rid of. This is a job that I had worked extremely hard for. Up to June 2020, I had spent twelve years in this field already. I was happy and quietly confident in my abilities. When I got the letter, I felt as though the world had closed in on me. I didn't know what to do.

Now, it is the first time that I will admit it openly but I spent almost three months in bed weeping. How did this happen to me? How did I end up without a job? Yes, while everyone was deadly worried about the pandemic and how we were going to get out of it, I was just buried in pain, feeling a lack of self-worth because I lost my job; the one thing that made me the happiest. I had foregone having a family. On nights when all my friends were out having a good time, my head was buried in books, the news, taking another exam, doing whatever I could to become the best in my field. I had worked hard since the very first day of college, so how did I end up being the one to be let go?

I didn't even tell my family and friends because I was ashamed of what they would think. Do you know what imposter syndrome is? Well, I had felt that for years in my work life, so the only thing I could think of was that everyone would now know that I am not as good as I seemed to be. So, with no job, I had nothing to do but bury myself in sorrow.

One day as I was in the shower preparing to go right back to bed just after noon, I had a thought. The question of why this was hurting so bad came to me and I realised that it wasn't just that I had lost my job, it was bigger than that. Though I was a valued team member, I didn't have something important that my two colleagues had. I wasn't confident enough. How could the company rely heavily on me when I didn't have the confidence to match my knowledge and skill base? It was then that I knew I had to fix it. I had to work on my confidence so that I would never be the one to be let go again. This is what prompted my journey and why I am able to write this book to help you.

Increasing your self-confidence is a process that requires constant reflection and effort. Making the required changes to boost your self-confidence can also make you more confident in your ability to facilitate meetings and network, interview, and even perform effectively in your current position. Self-confidence is vital in the working world, and this book discusses how you may increase your self-confidence so that you will continue to be a valued asset no matter what your role is at work. Additionally, by building up your confidence, you will be able to climb the career ladder and become the best version of you every step of the way.

By employing much of the strategies in this book, I interviewed at three different companies in the space of two weeks and was offered all three positions. For one of them, I was headhunted but I knew I did not want to work for that company. I still took the interview because I wanted to be sure that my perception was right—that I wasn't judging the book before reading its pages.

It came down to two companies, and after negotiations, I was able to secure an annual salary that is exactly thirty-one percent more than what I was earning at the job I lost. It is the same role with less responsibilities. However, I am a new me. I am more confident. I know my worth and I am confident enough to ask to be paid what I am worth. I was even able to negotiate starting two weeks later than requested. I was still working on my self-confidence and had a few more days before I could move to the next step, which involved employing strategies at work and with my new colleagues. I needed the time, so I asked and it was granted. The old me would not have even thought to request an additional day even if I had a scheduled surgery.

The other strategies I have added in this book are the ones that I now use in the workplace to help me in my role. I am sure that you will find many of them useful and might even be able to add to the list. If you are able to do the latter, do not hesitate to share them with me in your review of this book. As much as I want to know what you think and if these strategies are helping you, I am also opened to learning from you.

Make use of this book as often as you like. My advice is that you try to implement one or two things at a time. Do not overwhelm yourself and know that you can build your self-confidence one step and one day at a time. This book is just the start.

## What exactly is self-confidence, and how can you cultivate it?

An individual with high levels of self-confidence has faith in their ability to make sound judgments about themselves, make sound choices, and perform well under pressure—an attitude of confidence in one's ability to finish a job. Being self-aware and able to assess your strengths and limitations is a sign of self-confidence. Confidence in oneself is a distinct concept from self-esteem.

Despite the fact that the two terms are commonly used interchangeably, they refer to two distinct ideas. When we talk about self-esteem, we're talking about how well we think of ourselves, but when we talk about self-confidence, we're talking about how sure we are of our abilities to do specific tasks. The latter is how we present ourselves to others. This is what we will be discussing in this book, specifically how we present ourselves at work.

# Factors for Lack of Self-confidence

When I realised that my self-confidence was non-existent, my first resolve was to look internally to see what had caused this. I spent about a week looking at my career up to that point. Did something happen? What was my working environment like up to now? Was there ever a time when I was confident in the workplace?

After a week, I had journaled as much as I could to try to understand my circumstances. I took some time to look over my notes, then I turned to the internet. I wanted to know what others were saying about this and what other people's experience were. Luckily for me, I learned quickly that this was a problem that many people experienced and for different reasons. Some were similar to my own reasons but there were a lot of different ones that I did not identify with as well. In writing this book, I have collated the ones that I feel are more common based on my research, my own experience, and what I witnessed myself.

Many factors might contribute to your lack of self-confidence at work. These factors are often dictated by the environment in which you work as much as who you are as a person.

It's possible that you're working in a position that needs a skill set that you lack. For me, I needed to be able to present in front of groups but my fear of public speaking affected me in this regard.

It could also be that you're younger and less experienced than your co-workers. This in itself can cause you to feel fearful. The workplace is no different from the world in which we live. Just as much as you can be scared of an elder, you can be fearful of your superiors at work.

Additionally, if you're unsure about your capacity to succeed because you're a new employee or because you're afraid of losing your job, it's possible that you're too critical of yourself. This will affect the way you present yourself at work and thereby, your self-confidence.

One of the most frequent reasons why workers lose confidence is quite simply because of a negative connection with their boss. I have not experienced this in any of my role. However, this is something that I know happens for a fact and this book would not be complete without mentioning it. Reading this book, you might be in this exact position now. It is something that needs to be worked on, for as long as the connection is strained, that sense of uneasiness will persist and you will not gain back your self-confidence. Unfortunately, it might come down to you having to leave your job and find a position where you are more comfortable with your superiors.

Negative peer interactions may undermine one's self-esteem, particularly if there is a herd mentality. When one's self-esteem is impacted negatively, it can in turn affect their self-confidence. If someone sabotages you at work, for example, and you are afraid of your boss or manager—so you don't report the sabotage—over time, this sabotage can continue, resulting in your self-esteem being impacted. Before you know it, your self-confidence will be diminished entirely in the work environment. I identified with this and noticed that it started all the way back in high school.

As much as I am one now, I was nerdy in school. I realised early out that I wanted to be an accountant and took to my books. Because of this, I was made somewhat of an outcast. I was teased a lot and that affected my self-confidence severely. I did not care and until I did this exercise, I didn't realise that this was part of the problem as it continued on right into my career. I was known as the nerd from accounting and my only "friends" were from my department. I ate lunch alone, and unless we were talking about work, I was not included in conversations most of the time. I didn't mind because I was so used to it by now. However, it was affecting my work life and I needed to work on it and so I did.

Now, let's help you understand what has affected your self-confidence at work up to this point.

# Exercise 1

Take this time to assess your own situation and write down everything you can think of in response to the question below. I have left a few extra pages in case you want to take a few days like I did and journal. Journaling helped me to write down everything I felt over the course of seven days. I was then able to go through my writings and answer the ultimate question:

1. What has caused me to lose my self-confidence at work?

# Strategies to Revamp Your Self-confidence

Let me take this time to make one thing clear. If your self-esteem is high, in my opinion, your self-confidence will be just fine. Self-confidence is how you present yourself to everyone else. Therefore, it is very likely that if you feel good, you will present yourself positively. As a result, to work on your self-confidence, you must also work on your self-esteem. Experts recommend the following strategies for those who are struggling with low self-esteem or whose self-esteem has been shaken in some way:

### Keep your attention on yourself.
The easiest way to remain focused and productive is to ignore politics and the rumour mills. When you get involved in workplace rumour, especially if you help spread it, eventually the negative things that are said about others will also be said about you. A rumour can ruin your self-esteem and eventually your confidence, so stay away from engaging in them all together. A wonderful attitude and a long history of successful work are the best foundations for building confidence, not being a part of gossip with your colleagues.

### Make the most of your assets by recognizing and using them.
Getting clear on your talents and finding methods to incorporate those skills into what you do every day is one of the finest ways to create confidence—be engaged and enthusiastic when you lead from your strengths. Be confident in your abilities and accept where you need to make improvements.

Then, consider how you may put your best skills to use in your work environment to further your career. If your present position doesn't allow you to use your abilities to their fullest potential, consider looking for a new one.

## Recognize and address your areas of weakness.

If you have a weakness that is impacting your self-confidence, devise a strategy to lessen or eradicate it. Be aware of your flaws, but don't let them consume your thoughts and efforts. Working to improve yourself might give you more self-confidence in itself.

## Have faith in your own abilities.

Remember I mentioned imposter syndrome earlier? That is the easiest way to break down your self-confidence. You didn't get your job by chance. You were chosen because you have the skillset and potential necessary for the role, so believe in your abilities. Spend each day reminding yourself of this. Try to convince yourself, "I can do this," and believe it, even if it's hard to do. As an alternative to counting down the minutes till bedtime, you should advocate stating three affirmations aloud each night before turning in for the night. I implemented this and still do it almost two years later.

## Keep a close eye on your accomplishments.
You should keep a journal of your everyday successes. Start by creating a "to-do list." Your accomplishments will become more apparent as the things on your to-do list are crossed off one by one. At the end of this chapter, I will start you off on this. However, I do recommend that you implement this practice in your life for the long term. Each time you tick something off or complete a to-do list, it boosts your confidence and give you the feeling that you can keep going. It's an amazing feeling, trust me.

## Keep a digital "kudos file" of your accomplishments.

This follows on from the above point but is so important. Create a digital Kudos File on your computer or your phone. This is where you congratulate yourself and keep a record of what you have achieved. Your congratulations e-mails, notes to yourself about problems you've overcome, and thank-you letters from colleagues and friends are all kept here for safekeeping. For a self-reflection on your abilities and a personal pat on the back, consult this file often. When imposter syndrome kicks in and you start feeling as though you do not belong, go back to this file and look at all your achievements. It will also be helpful when you are looking for your next position as you can go back and show your new prospective employer what you have achieved in your career to date.

## Confidence might be shaky at times, so be aware of this.

Acknowledge that this is likely to happen and it happens to all of us, no matter how good we are at what we do. The aim of this book is not for us to have confidence one hundred percent of the time—I do not think this is possible. Instead, it is for us to be confident overall at work. However, from time to time, our confidence will be shaky.

You should wait twenty-four to forty-eight hours before replying to someone or making critical choices after becoming the victim of a mean-spirited remark or failing at something for example. This gives you the time to "pull it together" and get back to your confident self. Allow yourself the necessary time to calm down and look at all situations objectively. Where you do not have the time to allocate an extra day or two, take a walk or excuse yourself for a quick bathroom break. Look over your Kudos File and remember that you are good at what you do, then get back in there and be confident in giving your response.

## Seek out the support of others.

Ask individuals you admire what they believe are your three best assets. I found this very useful on my own journey and was amazed at the responses that I got from old colleagues, friends, and even family members. In the end, I had asked thirteen people and ended up with fourteen different assets. The most amazing part of this exercise for me was that most people, no matter what capacity they knew me in, named what I considered my best asset. Only two people did not give that answer.

I have created space in the exercise section for you to come up with your own list. Take the time to do this. Once you have that list, be sure that you are making the most of all those assets.

## Get feedback

This was extremely difficult for me because I started this process knowing very well that I lacked self-confidence at work. Therefore, I knew that I would get feedback on this. However, I was ready to take it on the chin because I wanted to become better. Get feedback on how you are doing from co-workers, friends, or even your boss/manager. Ask them to point out your positive attributes and areas where improvement is needed. In certain cases, we are more talented than we are aware of no matter how we feel about ourselves. This process will be extremely useful for you in the end.

## Attempt new things.

Being able to accomplish things that you previously thought were impossible can do wonders for your self-esteem and in turn improve your confidence. Take on initiatives that challenge you and allow you to utilize your abilities, and don't be afraid to take on new challenges. If your manager asks you to take on a particular task, it is likely that they know you can complete it effectively based on previous work. So, take on the challenge and do it to the best of your ability.

In my spare time, for example, I learn web development. It is something I caught onto a few years ago and find very interesting but I wouldn't change careers, so it is just something I do for fun. However, only a couple months or so ago, my company's site was giving problems and the tech team was having a hard time figuring it out. It is important that our site is always up and running and I understand this fully. While the team was busy trying to figure it out, I spotted what I thought the problem was. I spoke to one of the tech guys and he was appreciative that I did as he was then able to solve the problem quicker.

## You should cultivate an optimistic outlook.

To be "positive" does not necessarily imply being "happy." One can be sad and positive at the same time. I am naturally solution oriented, that's why I am successful in my field. However, the problems are numerous when it comes to accounting as I am sure it is for many other careers and sometimes it is hard to be optimistic. Nevertheless, it is extremely important and necessary in the workplace.

Naturally, you will be faced with problems on a daily basis. It is how you handle those problems that will make all the difference. No one likes a Debbie Downer, especially not at work. Therefore, it is important that you always present a positive attitude. Be optimistic.

When problems arise at work, be optimistic in helping to find solutions. Displaying this attitude is a sure way to foster team spirit and everyone likes to be around positivity.

Embracing this as a component of your "personal brand" can also help you project authority and self-assurance in the workplace. It is a sure way to promote your career growth.

# Exercise 2
## A. Affirmations

This was one of the very first strategies I implemented in this process. Here are my three affirmations that I used and still use today:

1. I am a *savage* accountant. I keep abreast of what is happening in my field and my knowledgebase and skillset serve me.
2. I am not an imposter. I am a great accountant and any company will be happy to have me as part of their team.
3. My colleagues appreciate me as part of the team and embrace my skills and my quirks alike.

Now, use the space below to write down your own affirmations. You do not have to stop at three.

## B. Weaknesses

Our weaknesses affect many aspects of our lives, including our self-confidence at work. As it relates to work, what are the weaknesses that I need to work on?

What can I do to eradicate each of the weaknesses I have identified above?

## C. Best Assets

Who are the three people that I can ask to list my best assets?

**Colleagues (3)**

 

**Friends (3)**

 

**Managers/boss/supervisor (3)**

 

Now that you have those assets written down, try to implement them in your work life to build on your confidence. Come back to this list from time to time to see how well you are doing in this regard or whether you have fallen off the wagon in implementing/making the best use of any of your assets.

## D. Feedback

Feedback is extremely important in this process. I know it can be daunting to hear what people really think of us and our work, but it is important for our growth and will help us build up our self-confidence in the long run.

It is time to get feedback from different people. You will need to focus on work, however, feedback from your friends will also be helpful in this process. For this exercise, you need feedback on **your confidence and how you present yourself in your job role.**

1. Get feedback from at least three co-workers and write them down below:

_____
_____
_____
_____
_____
_____
_____
_____
_____
_____
_____
_____
_____
_____
_____
_____
_____
_____

2. Now, get feedback from your immediate supervisor, boss, or manager.

3. Ask only friends who will be able to comment based on you talking to them about your work or them knowing you in this regard by some means. What feedback can they give you about your confidence and how you present yourself in your job role?

Now that you have everyone's feedback, what are the things that you need to work on?

### E. Attempt New Things

Over the next few weeks, and as you grow in your career, find ways to go above and beyond at work. If your manager does not ask you to do work that is not in your job description, it does not mean that you cannot do this. Try to volunteer to help out at work as it gives you the opportunity to interact with other colleagues and you get the chance to work on your self-confidence. (DO NOT offer to take on more work if you have not completed the tasks that are set in your job description as it will impact your position negatively.)

What can I do this week to attempt new things at work?

## F. To-do List

Create your to do list below. I have left enough space for at least a full day or two; it might even be enough for a week. You can use the extra pages at the back of the book to create new lists each week.

Write down the things that you have do over the next day or week. Tick them off as you complete each of them and celebrate when you have completed all your tasks.

# Self-confidence in the Workplace: a Few Real-world Examples

In the workplace, a few instances of self-confidence include the following:

- Doing what is right, regardless of what others think.
- Having the courage to go out of your comfort zone and take on new tasks.
- Recognizing and addressing your own personal shortcomings.
- Acknowledging and accepting credit for your own work. Never allow others to present your work as their own.
- Acknowledging your talents and flaws as part of who you are.
- Confidence in delivering your views and ideas at a meeting. Raise your hand and ask questions if you need to. It is better to ask when you are unsure.

# How to Become More Self-confident at Work

At this stage, we have gone over what a lack of self-confidence looks like and how it can affect us in the work place. By now, you have completed a few of the exercises at the least and you have a better understanding of what affects your confidence. You should have also taken steps to get feedback from others about how you present yourself at work and in your job role in general. Now, let's look at the steps you need to take to become more confident at work.

Before I get into it, I want to let you know that these strategies can be applied to any aspect of your life. The more confident I grew at work, the more confident I became in life. I started implementing many of the strategies in my life in general and saw results that I wouldn't have thought possible before. For example, and it is definitely a discussion for another book, I asked my crush out after knowing her for almost ten years and she said yes to the first date. We have been almost inseparable since and celebrated our first year's anniversary this March. As I said though, that's for another book.

Employ the below strategies to boost your self-confidence in the workplace:

## Keep an open mind and be willing to give new ideas a go.
Taking on new initiatives as a volunteer may not only help you learn new abilities but can also boost your self-esteem at work. Don't hesitate to take on a new role or enrol in a new training program. I have so many certifications that many would consider unnecessary, however, on many of the courses, I have learned something new that I find useful. Invest in yourself and your professional growth.

### Participate fully in the process of evaluating your own performance.
Asking for direct input on your strengths and flaws might be beneficial if your employer conducts performance appraisals. As a next step, identify the exact actions that will help.

Recognize your own positive and negative attributes and work on improving them. Accepting feedback and constructive criticism from others is as vital as recognizing your own strengths and weaknesses. I do recommend that you do this continuously and outside of the ones your work will schedule for you.

### Give yourself some breathing room before taking on new endeavours.
Developing self-confidence requires advanced planning. If you fail to plan, you will likely be nervous which is counterproductive. Do what is necessary and prepare ahead of time, particularly when you have an imminent assignment or presentation to do. This allows you to remain calm and confident when you are presenting your work.

### Do not be ashamed of your individuality.
You may easily compare your own talents to those of colleagues, but you should also be aware of the contrasts between you and them and the ways in which they contribute to your advantages. What are some of the ways in which you are different from your colleagues or team members, and how do these distinctions contribute to the company's overall goals?

### Maintaining a sense of perspective is key to achieving your objectives.
Confidence may be bolstered by successfully completing tasks and exceeding deadlines. The abbreviation SMART refers to objectives that are Specific, Measurable, Achievable, Realistic, and Timely (SMART). There are many books out there as well as information on the internet that can help you understand this better. Look into it and see how best you can

implement the SMART goal setting strategy to help you build on your confidence at work. Remember, being prepared lessens the chances of you being nervous, so preparation is indeed key.

### Analyse the language you use to communicate to yourself.
Self-doubt is a common result of dwelling on the negative. Make an effort to pay attention to your own self-talk. If you were in the same circumstance as a colleague, imagine what you would say to them and say it to yourself.

### Make friends with your co-workers.
Building trust in the workplace is another way to improve one's self-confidence. By helping others, you may strengthen your friendships at work and thus the working environment. As a result, they will be more willing to assist you if you ever need it.

### Quiet your inner critic.
This is linked to positive self-talk but is so important to be addressed on its own. It can also be helpful to identify where your self-doubts are coming from. Ask yourself, "Why do I think I can't do this? What is that that makes me think that I can't do well or succeed?" Once you are able to answer these questions, you can develop means and ways to overcome this way of thinking. In essence, you can quiet these thoughts and replace them with more positive ones.

### Take care of your physical and mental health.
Studies show that maintaining your physical and mental health outside of the workplace is also important to self-confidence in the workplace. If you feel good about yourself in general, as I said earlier, you are able to exude that.

## Define confidence in terms of what exactly it means to you.

In order to develop self-confidence, it is important to understand what it is. What does self-confidence mean to you? Think about the attributes of self-confidence specific to a work environment. Perhaps you might identify a manager or co-worker who you consider to be confident. What about them makes you believe they are confident? How do they speak? How do they respond to questions? How do they present themselves during meetings? Consider these questions as you move into the exercise section of this chapter.

# Exercise 3

### A. Definition of self-confidence.

What does self-confidence mean to me?

_____
_____
_____
_____
_____
_____
_____
_____

### B. Embrace your individuality

What are some of the ways in which I am different from my colleagues or team members, and how do these distinctions contribute to my company's overall goals?

_____
_____
_____
_____
_____
_____
_____
_____
_____
_____
_____
_____
_____
_____
_____

## C. Self-improvement

Are there any courses or trainings that I can enrol on?

How much will each of these costs and when can I enrol?

### D. Positive self-talk

List up to 10 negative phrases that you say to yourself below and replace each of them with positive self-talk.

Here's an example:

Negative: Alejandro, you are never going to get anywhere if you can't stand up and speak in front of a crowd. How hard is it?

Positive: I understand that it's difficult for you to speak publicly. However, it is important for you to do this report, so take a deep breath and do your best. With a little practice, you will get better over time.

Now, go ahead and do the same below.

### E. Performance Appraisal

I recommend that you use the pages available at the back of this book to do an appraisal at least every quarter. Notice that you are doing this over time to gauge how much you improve as time goes by.

What are my core responsibilities and the challenges I face in carrying them out?

_____
_____
_____
_____
_____
_____
_____
_____
_____
_____
_____
_____
_____
_____
_____
_____
_____

What can I do to address those challenges?

_____
_____
_____
_____
_____
_____
_____
_____
_____

Only come back to this after a month or so. What strategies have I employed that are working and which ones need changing?

## F. SMART

Have you already read up on the SMART goal setting technique ? If not, go ahead and do so then come back to this task.

Now, using the SMART strategy, prepare for your next major task at work.

# Conclusion

My hope is that you have gained something from this book. It is not easy to gain or build self-confidence at work, however, it is possible to do so over time and, in the end, it will so be worth it. For me, once my confidence at work started improving, it showed up in other aspects of my life too. In essence, you will experience growth in different aspects of your life which will help you grow overall.

All of the discussion in the book comes down to the point that, when you know what you're excellent at and the value you bring to the table, you'll be confident in yourself and your actions.

You'll come off as more self-assured: people will take your words and actions more seriously if they sense your conviction. You'll be able to go forward in your company and in your career as a result of this.

You'll get more done: You'll be more inclined to take on tough but achievable tasks. Your comfort zone will be expanded, and you'll be motivated to set and accomplish new objectives as a result. Both of these traits are highly prized amongst highly effective professionals. You'll gain the confidence of your employers and be recognized as a leader who can inspire others by demonstrating your ability to take on responsibility and lead projects successfully.

You'll be able to express yourself more clearly. Confidence gives you the ability to talk clearly and succinctly. Confident communicators are able to explain their intentions to customers and co-workers in a concise and direct way. Advancement in one's job is impossible without good verbal and written communication skills.

Interpersonal skills, professionalism, and passion are all results of self-confidence that companies want in their workforce. No matter how smart or skilled you are at your job, if you lack the necessary confidence, it might be difficult for employers to trust you in your role.

Finally, organizations gain from confident workers since they are more positive contributors, more productive and motivating, and excellent role models. Employees in customer-facing or sales roles who are self-assured also have a significant impact on how customers see the company.

Shift your perspective: People who aren't sure of themselves worry a lot about what other people think of them. Instead, they need to think about how their actions affect others. You'll become more productive as a result since you'll realize that what counts most is what you do, not what others do to you.

Don't hide it under the rug when you accomplish something good or achieve something. Acknowledge your successes. Recognize and congratulate yourself, even if the accomplishment is little. Make sure your supervisor is aware of any accomplishments you've had. Make sure you're not pushing your own barrow by overestimating your accomplishments.

Confidence is key: 'A picture tells a thousand words' is a well-known proverb. Think about it now. What do you think about your appearance? What impression do you leave on the people around you when you enter a room? What are you trying to communicate with your body language? What can potential customers or co-workers learn about you before you ever open your mouth to speak? As you can see, a confident demeanour is critical. Be conscious of your body language and how it communicates with others. Think about how you're putting yourself out there. Be sure you're moving with purpose when you're moving across a room.

The greatest method to stand out in today's employment market is to demonstrate your self-confidence in the workplace. There are many people with the exact same skillset as you, so stand out by being the best version of yourself.

# Notes